THE BOOK OF THE

LORD NELSONS

A Photographic Accompaniment

Notes by Richard Derry

30856 LORD ST VINCENT at Eastleigh, with BR Standard 2-6-0 in the background. Photograph The Transport Treasury.

IRWELL PRESS Ltd.

An Evening to Remember

Lord Nelson 861 was involved in tests over the Salisbury to Exeter main line, together with N15 789 and Merchant Navy 21C14, in September 1946. For a young teenage admirer of the Nelsons, residing in Exeter, this presented a marvellous opportunity to study one of the class locally. So for several evenings Exmouth Junction shed was the mandatory venue for seeing black liveried LORD ANSON after it had brought down the 12.50pm from Waterloo.

On 19 September 1946 I was gazing at the engine while it was waiting to turn and a considerate driver asked: 'Are you interested in this locomotive?' Needless to say the answer was a prompt yes, whereupon he invited me up to the footplate with him while the Nelson was turned, ran back and reversed into the shed yard for next day's return working. My driver friend soon departed leaving me on the driver's seat and imagining I was hurtling along at speeds to make MALLARD's exploits look like it was going backwards! I was brought back to earth when two bowler hatted gentleman came aboard; I fully expected to get my come uppance but instead they merely nodded politely in my direction – perhaps imagining I was the privileged son of an even higher up bowler. Anyway one of them proceeded to wield a long handled shovel with a flaming oily rag around the inside of the firebox. I gathered a steam blow had been reported but they concluded they could let it go.

While this was going on Urie Arthur 744 MAID OF ASTOLAT was alongside displaying a NOT TO BE MOVED board and the reason was clear to see. The rear left-hand coupling rod was missing and the loco was in steam with safety valves just lifting and making the eerie moaning sound associated with Urie boilers when blowing off point was approached. In due course a gang of fitters appeared carrying the coupling rod which they soon had in place, with fastenings secure and the King Arthur ready for its next duty. An evening to remember!

Eric Youldon, Exeter, 2005.

First published in the United Kingdom in 2005
by Irwell Press Limited, 59A, High Street, Clophill,
Bedfordshire MK45 4BE

THE BOOK OF THE LORD NELSONS
A Photographic Accompaniment

Picture This

The last eight years has seen the 'Book Of' series of locomotive studies develop into something of a library devoted to more and more of the principal BR express classes. Since 1997 there has been:

More than that, as a sort of *de facto* journal, there have been (or there are in preparation) a number of paperback *Photographic Accompaniments* to further celebrate these famous classes. These include:

Now it's the Lord Nelsons' turn and once again the purpose is to serve up further photographs for this fascinating class. Again, the idea is to accompany, supplement and complement the 'parent' volume, *The Book of the Lord Nelson 4-6-0s*. As pointed out therein, the Lord Nelsons seemed something of a fearsome prospect, such was their reputation for 'difficulties' of the engine picking kind. I'd last seen one (a glum LORD ANSON) in 1962 and was barely acquainted with the class compared with, say, the Britannias, the other BR Standards and the various Bulleid Pacifics, which I came to know so well both throughout the 1960s and in preservation since. All of these classes have since seen their own 'Books Of' with Irwell Press. Among the Nelsons, we were warned, 'no single engine was the same as another' and indeed this

'The most powerful passenger locomotive in the country'. LORD NELSON at Nine Elms (the blackened frame of the old coal shelter is in the background) equipped with the indicator shelter for evaluation on the Western Section, after running in from Eastleigh. Indicator drive from the crosshead can be discerned. During its prolonged evaluation before the 'production' run of Nelsons commenced, LORD NELSON was engaged in all sorts of out of the ordinary work, which further removed it from the general day to day experience of your average crew. It was often on exhibition – most notably perhaps alongside the old Brighton 0-4-2 GLADSTONE at Brighton in May 1927. It began revenue earning service with the 11am boat train from Victoria on 16 May 1927 but a typical 'special' the following year, which would have meant days of preparation, was taking the King and Queen of Afghanistan's train. The five Pullmans from Waterloo to Weymouth Junction (for the Afghan King to visit the fleet at Portland) at just over 142 miles was the longest non-stop run ever made on the Southern. What locomotive would do, other than LORD NELSON? Photograph H.C. Casserley, courtesy R.M. Casserley.

LORD NELSON was much in demand for shows around the country and this shimmering, burnished beauty would grace any gathering of locomotives. This is Wavertree Park, Liverpool on 7 September 1930 and E850 LORD NELSON looks gorgeous – except that it is E861 LORD ANSON in disguise! Photograph H.C. Casserley, courtesy R.M. Casserley.

seemed a daunting prospect. It was Eric Youldon to the rescue, as recounted in *The Book of the Lord Nelson 4-6-0s*. The Nelsons it turned out, when you thought about, weren't really better or worse than most other classes when it came to the 'engine picking' side of things. Though a particular locomotive might have highly singular features, this was only a matter of degree; a degree, moreover, that was quite comparable to other passenger classes. The text of these *Accompaniments* can only be brief of course and what follows is but an echo of what is set out in *The Book of the Lord Nelson 4-6-0s*, yet I hope it will serve to outline the main features of the class and the alterations and additions that befell them, besides encouraging the reader of course, to buy both books!

References: *Maunsell's Nelsons* by D.W. Winkworth (Allen & Unwin); *The Schools 4-4-0s* by D.W. Winkworth (Allen & Unwin); *Locos of the LSWR* Vol. 2 D.L. Bradley (RCTS); *Locos of the SR* Vol. 1 D.L. Bradley (RCTS); *LSWR Locos, Urie Classes*. D.L. Bradley (Wild Swan); *The Arthurs, Nelsons and Schools of the Southern*, by S.C. Townroe (Ian Allan).

These works have been ransacked from stem to stern (with both eyes! – readers will appreciate the Nelsonian image) and while it is always difficult to uncover anything that is *wholly* new we take some quiet satisfaction from the photographs and the contemporary references. And the odd hole, strap, hook, bolt pattern or whatever, hitherto

overlooked in the literature, has been uncovered.

Thanks are due, in especial, to Eric Youldon; also to D.W. Winkworth, Ian Sixsmith, Chris Hawkins, Martin Smith, Peter Groom, R.C. Riley, Gavin Morrison and Ronald Wilkinson, Eddie Scrumpter, Bryan Wilson and Alan Wild.

****

It was R.E.L. Maunsell who was responsible for the Lord Nelsons. Appointed CME, he had to develop a design able to run over all the Southern's varied and often restricted main routes with heavy trains at speeds approaching 60mph average. This immediately meant a tussle with the Civil Engineer and Maunsell probably spent more effort pacifying his Civil Engineering counterpart than in actually designing his new locomotive. What this meant was that LORD NELSON, when it finally emerged from Eastleigh in works grey in August 1926, represented a minor miracle, one of forcing a hugely significant increase in power in a 4-6-0 type with a minimal increase in weight. Maunsell deserves acclaim for a feat of minor genius in getting a power/weight outcome in his Lord Nelsons that was simply startling. LORD NELSON was barely a ton heavier than an Arthur yet for a driving axle weight increase of less than half a ton, the Nelson provided an increase in tractive effort from 25,321lbs to 33,510lbs, almost exactly a third.

Moreover, the locomotive burst into a PR world very different from today's, in which the Monarchy was revered and heroes were generals, admirals and scout leaders and there was glamour in Ocean Liners and express trains. No little part of the effort put into the design was to ensure that LORD NELSON could be claimed as 'the most powerful passenger engine in the country' and much play was made of this. It was no accident that the inaugural public run was on the Atlantic Coast Express. The new Lord Nelson class was designed to operate over all the main lines of the Southern and in keeping with the 'PR' concerns of the time, the catchy phrase '500 tons at 55mph' came into currency. *The Railway Gazette* account of the new engine's unveiling (a truncated version follows below) was extensive, acclamatory and just what the Southern PR people wanted:

'In point of tractive power development, the engine marks an advance upon the 'King Arthur' class, and, indeed on this, the commonly accepted basis of power computation for steam locomotives, it ranks as the most powerful passenger engine in Great Britain,

'The steam passages and piping are laid out to advantage in such a way as to secure free circulation of the steam to and from the cylinders.

'An interesting feature of the design in this connection is that there are eight separate impulses per revolution of the coupled wheels, this resulting from a special disposition of the crank pins,

Nelsons in original condition, at Petts Wood in the boat train heyday of the class; 857 LORD HOWE on 28 March 1929 and 853 SIR RICHARD GRENVILLE (with six wheel tender) on 20 July the same year. They seem strange to our eyes now for it's not a look we are used to. Oddly, without the smoke deflectors, so distinctively Southern, the Nelsons certainly had that air of bulk you'd expect from 'the most powerful passenger locomotive in Great Britain'. 853 has the extended lamp iron seen again in later years with Britannias on the Golden Arrow. Photograph H.C. Casserley, courtesy R.M. Casserley.

E852 SIR WALTER RALEIGH as built in July 1928 with six wheel tender – it was paired with it for just sixteen months.

Boat train working again, with 859 LORD HOOD. The year is not known but the Urie type tender was replaced in 1932. The 'Continental Link' that operated out of Stewarts Lane saw its Lord Nelsons employed most intensively in the summer when the traffic was heaviest. Works visits, so far as was possible, were programmed for the winter months and throughout 'the season' a Battersea Nelson would be considered fully engaged on a daily job to the coast and back. This did not allow mileages to accumulate rapidly and though it was quite possible for a Nelson to work two round trips to Dover or Folkestone in a day, this was not usual. Perhaps timetabling patterns made it awkward. Photograph F.H. Stingemore, The Transport Treasury.

E860 LORD HAWKE in original condition, at Nine Elms on 22 March 1930; Urie type tender, original intricate standard Maunsell or 'sage' green livery. This was the engine originally fitted with the longer boiler – hence the absence of a piano' at the front. The engine (compare with others) has the original 'deep-set' bogie, a feature never revealed before in books and magazines, until that is, *The Book Of* and its ilk. If not quite an engine picking nugget, then at least a chrome plated revelation! Photograph H.C. Casserley, courtesy R.M. Casserley.

by means of which the individual exhausts from both ends of all cylinders occur separately instead of the usual arrangement of synchronised exhausts giving four beats per revolution of the wheels in four-cylinder engines having quartered cranks.

'The arrangement provides a more uniform torque and also more regular firebox draught than is possible with the customary system. The revolving and reciprocating parts have been made as light as possible by using a special high tensile steel, and the advantage gained thereby is also reflected in the lightness of the balance weights in the wheels.

'In this engine, Mr Maunsell has produced a well-designed and highly-efficient development of the 4-6-0 type in accordance with British practice standards. The appearance of the engine is excellent to a degree, and judging by its performance during the inaugural trip on Tuesday last, October 12, when the engine took the 'Atlantic Coast' express from Waterloo to Salisbury, it has a considerable reserve of power in hand when working trains of between 400 and 450 tons weight. Actually, the engine has been constructed to haul trains of 500 tons at an average speed of 55 miles per hour, the heaviest trains on the Southern Railway at the present time being from 425 to 450 tons.

****

Ten more Lord Nelsons were delivered between June 1928 and April 1929; all were from Eastleigh to Order No.E157

(LORD NELSON had been E124) as follows:

E851 SIR FRANCIS DRAKE
E852 SIR WALTER RALEIGH
E853 SIR RICHARD GRENVILLE
E854 HOWARD OF EFFINGHAM
E855 ROBERT BLAKE
E856 LORD St VINCENT
E857 LORD HOWE
E858 LORD DUNCAN
E859 LORD HOOD
E860 LORD HAWKE

The last five Nelsons were built from September through to November 1929 (the 'E' went in 1931):

E861 LORD ANSON
E862 LORD COLLINGWOOD
E863 LORD RODNEY
E864 SIR MARTIN FROBISHER
E865 SIR JOHN HAWKINS

****

'The most powerful passenger engine in the country' never really lived up to expectations and to the end of steam was overshadowed by its exact contemporaries, the GW Castles and the (admittedly rebuilt and reinvigorated) LMS Royal Scots. Crucially (see below) these were built in substantial numbers compared to Maunsell's mere sixteen – 'enough to operate only a single Link'. In power, they certainly can be said to have 'superseded' the King Arthurs but, as fine an engine as the King Arthur was, this simple fact hardly ushers in the

Lord Nelsons to the locomotive Hall of Fame.

Tractive effort, moreover, is misleading; it was boiler and firebox – especially the latter – that produced power, not tractive efforts. It wasn't so much that a Nelson was disappointing, as a matter of expectations being unrealistically high. A dispassionate study of the Nelson and the Arthur shows that the former was unlikely to better the latter by much more than 10% in terms of steam production and thus performance.

Tractive effort was one thing, performance was another and it must have been demoralising to hear of men (perplexed by the split level firebox and unable to get the best out of it) expressing *a preference* for an Arthur on many jobs! Maunsell, incidentally, carried on the building of King Arthurs at this period, improving the earlier Urie ones to hold the line before the new Lord Nelson class was developed. What he did was provide an engine many crews would take *instead* of a Nelson, given the choice. The irony was that, years later, the Southern crews took to the BR Standard Class 5s (with their split grates!) like ducks to water.

Though ultimately failing (if judged as a class that was intended to be the front rank of Southern passenger power) the Lord Nelsons were nonetheless an excellent design. Certainly E850 LORD NELSON was an acme of that development process that gave us all the great designs, the squeezing of more and more power into an existing profile (the Princess Coronations and Britannias were similar milestones).

That the Nelsons did not make a sustained impact is entirely explicable, though it is only possible to outline the circumstances here. There weren't enough of them for a start; sixteen engines (though it had been intended at one time that there would be twenty-six of them) was, as has been mentioned, sufficient only for one Link, on the Eastern Section at Stewarts Lane, with the rest left sprinkled among the King Arthurs on the Western Section. Despite this several Nelsons were stored in winter – an result, perhaps, of the Southern policy of allocating locos for days of 'maximum use'. Whatever, it seems odd that they were never concentrated at one shed in the 1930s.

Though they were capable of excellent individual performances they were very different to fire compared to existing Arthurs (the split level firebox was new to the SR) and not enough men got them regularly enough. A 'difficult' reputation was acquired very quickly and such a millstone was rarely thrown off. Maunsell's careful introduction, designed to iron out faults on the prototype, paradoxically made it worse. A single locomotive (we only have to think of 71000 DUKE OF GLOUCESTER) was of little real use to your average Operating Department – 'more of an embarrassment' in fact as

Winkworth puts it – because it can have no impact on schedules, while crews only meet with it now and then. Every time they work it, it's new-fangled and awkward and the downward spiral of unfamiliarity/bad experience/dislike is set in place. A disappointing early record of mechanical failure diminished the Nelson's reputation further and much of the work they did was a long way from the '500 tons at 55mph' aim. As stated in *The Book of the Lord Nelson 4-6-0s*: *LORD NELSON's fate was to be around long enough for everyone to get to dislike it. When the rest of the class came, there were still not sufficient numbers to firmly establish the Nelsons as the new generation of top express power.*

The 'best' years of the Nelsons were the 1930s when they worked so many of the principal boat trains, though some workings went over to pairs of 4-4-0s. Bulleid's alterations in the 1930s and 1940s – modified tenders, new cylinders with different ports and passages, Lemaître exhausts, new grate and ashpan arrangements – made the Lord Nelsons a much better proposition but the War abruptly took away any opportunity to shine, in the public sense at least. After the War, Merchant Navy Pacifics were the principal express engines while light Pacifics were flooding in to 'fill up the corners'. From that time on the Nelsons were retained partly to cover the extraordinary summer Saturday peaks encountered on the Southern – though they were particularly useful when Pacific availability fluctuated.

By February 1940 the Nelsons were concentrated at Nine Elms; two years later a number went to Bournemouth to replace Schools 4-4-0s and the class finished the War divided between two sheds, Bournemouth and Nine Elms. Later the whole class was concentrated again, at Eastleigh. Through the 1950s, 'the most powerful passenger locomotive in the country' formed the 'Second Division' of the Bournemouth and Salisbury lines, along with the Schools, various other ex-LSW 4-6-0s and the BR Standard Class 5 4-6-0s. The Nelsons were 7P in the BR scheme of things but much of the work could hardly compare with what many similarly classified 7P locomotives were doing elsewhere – Royal Scots, A3s, Castles and so on. They just about kept their own but as the 1950s wore on they were increasingly sidelined; despite this the Nelsons maintained a good level of reliability, were kept in respectable condition, did good mileage between repairs and generally got all the various modifications and additions that were applied at the time. Given Townroe's conviction that they were obsolete by the time the BR Standard 4-6-0s arrived, this was not bad going!

857 LORD HOWE in the wartime black, at Bournemouth West on 18 April 1943 during the second period of the special boiler – this time without the bevelled smoke deflectors. It had apparently been equipped with a thermic syphon by this time. Photograph G.O.P. Pearce.

Engine Picking the Lord Nelsons – A Brief Guide

As is usual for these *Accompaniments*, a brief version of the 'engine picker's guide' is reproduced, a much condensed version of that in the 'parent' book. There was a sequence of modifications to the Lord Nelsons; Maunsell made some fundamental departures from the originals (though the results were piffling) while Bulleid of course sought to bring them up to scratch with respect to steaming. He seems to have more or lost interest once his Pacifics were on the go...

Driving Wheel Diameter
E859 LORD HOOD appeared with 6ft 3in driving wheels, instead of 6ft 7in. There was no discernible difference in working, despite an indicated increase in tractive effort, either on the Eastern or Western Sections; nonetheless LORD HOOD kept the 'small' wheels throughout its life.

Long Boiler
E860 LORD HAWKE came out with a longer boiler and once again effects were minimal. The Nelsons had a noticeable 'piano front' between the frames but E860 had a flat front, prefiguring later developments for the class as a whole when Bulleid had improved cylinders fitted.

Tenders
LORD NELSON's bogie tender was an impressive thing, flat sided, five tons and 5,000 gallons with prominent vacuum reservoirs at the rear. The rest

came to get something similar but not before some variation occurred.
The first 'production' ten E851-E860, were to get six wheel tenders intended for the King Arthurs they replaced in the works ordering but some, E851, E854, E855, E856 and E857, went to the Western Section and had to have second-hand flat sided 5,000 gallon bogie tenders off S15s. Of the rest, only E852 and E853 got six wheel 4,000 gallon tenders; E858, E859 and E860 came out with second-hand Urie 5,000 gallon tenders, distinguishable by their curved top edges.

The last five, E861-E865, had flat sided 5,000 gallon bogie tenders. The smaller 4,000 gallon tenders were inadequate and the two on E852 and E853 were replaced by 5,000 gallon tenders with curved top edges in December 1929 and February 1930 respectively. So five, E852, E853, E858, E859 and E860 then had the tenders with curved tops; these were replaced by flat sided tenders in 1931 and 1932 so that by the summer of that year all the Nelsons had 5,000 gallon flat sided tenders. They were numbered 1000-1015, in series with the engines, 850-865.

We know the Nelsons best with their high sided tenders – these were the results of fitting 'self trimming bunkers' to make sure the coal moved forward on the road and thereby make the Fireman's job easier. Bulleid had the work done, beginning with 852 SIR WALTER RALEIGH in November 1937.

It was complete with 863 LORD RODNEY at the end of 1940.

Lamp Irons
Before smoke deflectors appeared, the two top lamp irons projected out from the smokebox rim; with deflectors the irons were moved up slightly but the discs projected out and obscured the Driver's forward sighting, so they were moved again 'inboard', to the smokebox door itself. At the same time, it would seem, a small handle on the right-hand side of the door (looking from the cab) was removed to make way for the right-hand iron. Afterwards you opened the door by grasping the lamp iron.

Wheel Balances
The Lord Nelsons had 135Ú crank settings, which gave a unique eight separate exhaust beats per revolution of the coupled wheels. Maunsell had 865 SIR JOHN HAWKINS revert to the traditional 90Ú which rendered it identifiable from the rest even as it came into sight, from its conventional four exhaust beats per revolution. It also had a different set of wheel balances, much more prominent than on the others. No obvious effects were detected, though it was ever after lumbered with a reputation for heavier coal consumption.

Double Chimney
862 LORD COLLINGWOOD emerged with a double chimney and modified Kylchap in-line twin exhausts in August 1934. It was not the success that it was

There's something at the bottom of the garden... In a stirring and smoky side-on portrait, 858 LORD DUNCAN as seen from the *jardin chez* Casserley, 15 October 1933. Photograph H.C. Casserley, courtesy R.M. Casserley.

elsewhere and offered no particularly obvious improvement. No.865 SIR JOHN HAWKINS got a double Kylchap in March 1938 and the arrangement on 862 LORD COLLINGWOOD was amended; both were tested on the Bournemouth line showing some improvement, it is said. It was not pronounced enough to prompt a general fitting.

Lemaître Exhaust
The Nelsons are best known for that wonderful Lemaître 'bowl'. Following various experiments Bulleid had them all done in 1939.

'Pacific' Boiler
In 1937 857 LORD HOWE appeared with a unique taper boiler with round top firebox no.1063, carrying it from 1937 to 1941 and again from 1943 to 1945.

Snifting Valves
There were prominent 'snifting valves' on either side of the chimney, except for the taper boiler on 857 LORD HOWE, which had one only, behind the chimney. They were removed between 1947 and 1949.

Speed Recorders/Speedometers
All the Nelsons were equipped with the Flaman speed recorders, which provided a record on a paper roll as well as an indication for the Driver. It was driven off the right-hand rear coupled wheel. They were removed as a wartime economy and never refitted. The Nelsons were included in the BR programme of fitting speedometers, begun in 1959. This was the familiar equipment attached to the left-hand rear driving wheel but not all survived long enough to get it.

New Cylinders
Bulleid rearranged the grates and ashpans too, for better airflow, then he renewed the cylinders; with this the Nelsons had been more or less rebuilt and they were a much better engine. Sadly the War meant they'd never 'shine' in the public sense and they would soon be overshadowed by the Pacifics in any case. With variations, the new cylinders meant the smokebox was extended slightly so that the 'piano' front over the cylinders disappeared, and the steam pipes no longer projected through the smoke deflectors; instead, they were out of sight behind them:

850: new cylinders 3/42, loses piano front
851: new cylinders 6/39 but non-standard, retains piano front
852: new cylinders 3/40, loses piano front
853: new cylinders 2/58, loses piano front
854: new cylinders 11/46, loses piano front
855: new cylinders 12/40, loses piano front
856: new cylinders 7/40, loses piano front
857: new cylinders 10/39, piano front already gone
858: new cylinders 1/51, loses piano front
859: new cylinders 12/46, loses piano front
860: new cylinders 12/39, piano front already gone
861: new cylinders 8/43, loses piano front
862: new cylinders 4/40, loses piano front
863: no new cylinders, retains piano front to the end
864: new cylinders 5/48, loses piano front
865: new cylinders 9/40, loses piano front

AWS
Automatic Warning System again came late and again not all Nelsons lasted long enough to get it. The battery box was on the left-hand side on the running plate, above the new speedometer. Some got the AWS but not the speedometer (though where fitted, it was always at the same time as the AWS) while one, 30865, got neither.

Livery
The 'E' prefix merely denoted an engine allocated to Eastleigh for repairs and was dropped in 1931.

The standard SR 'Maunsell' green, otherwise called 'sage green' (see Table for dates) had black and white lining with yellow lettering. It was intricately done, with lined out green cylinders (bands front and aft) and footsteps and even lining on the green 'splashers' over the bogie wheels.

The Nelsons had cab numberplates; like the name plates, the background was painted red. Tenders had SOUTHERN with the engine number painted below.

Two, 855 and 862, appeared in 1938 with panels on the cylinders instead of conventional lining.

The front number was painted on the bufferbeam, prefaced by 'No.' on the other side of the drawhook. The 'No.' was dropped when the 'E' prefix appeared and then reappeared when the 'E' was dropped in turn in 1931. In this second form, the 'No.' had the underline set higher, with a dot underneath it. Smoke deflectors were black, like the smokebox.

The olive green of 1938, which appeared on some engines, had yellow and dark green lining with cylinders and smoke deflectors black. The number plates were replaced by numbers painted on the cab side; 'No.' was finally dropped.

Generally speaking, malachite green followed, then wartime black and malachite again (again see Table for dates and individual sequences). Lining variations were, well, listen to Bradley: *there were so many variations of the theme that the only features common to all were the large gilt buffer beam numerals, SOUTHERN on the tenders and cab numerals.*

Three got a trial BR apple green livery in 1948 (it weathered poorly) and the Nelsons avoided the BR blue; all soon got the BR dark (in reality GW) green.

***

With tenders carrying the number as well as the engine, it was bound to happen... 853 passes Bromley on 14 July 1935 gaily towing the tender of 863. Photograph H.C. Casserley, courtesy R.M. Casserley.

Tender rear panel, 5,000 gallon straight sided, on 857 LORD HOWE at Dover shed, 29 April 1934. Photograph H.C. Casserley, courtesy R.M. Casserley.

The big-boilered 857 LORD HOWE, at Salisbury shed – a place where Nelson were not photographed all that often – at an unknown date. It had this taper boiler no.1063 (said to be the prototype for a putative Pacific/goods 4-8-0) for two separate periods, 1937-1941 and 1943-1945. The boiler had a round top firebox, combustion chamber (indicated by the long row of firebox plugs) and 'Sinuflo' superheater rather than a Maunsell one and looked even bigger than it was because of the reduced chimney and dome (the boiler was pitched higher than on the other Nelsons). Its size also warranted an adaptation to the deflectors, variously described as 'cranked', 'bevelled' and so on. For this boiler's second innings, standard deflectors were employed. The photographer's 'camera case' (an old suitcase) sits in the foreground. Photograph The Transport Treasury.

The SR malachite was a sublime livery and highly distinctive. A similar view of 864 SIR MARTIN FROBISHER appears in *The Book of the Lord Nelson 4-6-0s*: there is no date but it would be 1939, when the engine first got this livery, along with the Lemaître exhaust. When malachite appeared again, after the war, the paintwork did not include the footsteps (as visible here). Cylinders black and unlined, panel on smoke deflector. The pattern of studs on the right-hand cabside indicate internal fittings connected with the Flaman speed recorder. Photograph The Transport Treasury.

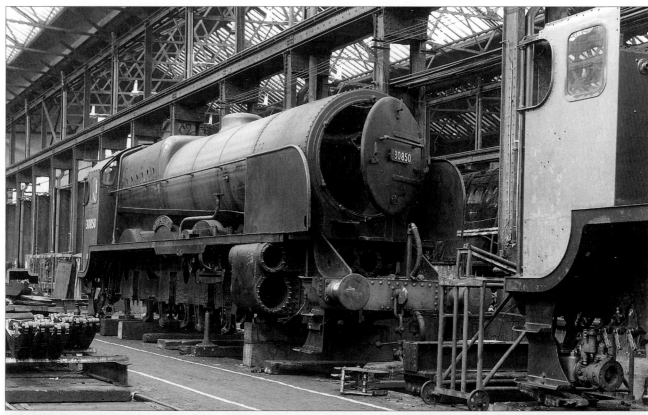

LORD NELSON and a compatriot (it would be LORD HOOD) in Eastleigh Works, 14 May 1955. Bradley in his RCTS volume produces mileage figures which put the Nelsons in a markedly favourable light, though it is hard to make direct comparisons, given differences in the type of work done and the repair regimes on the Regions. The Nelsons managed 93,000 miles between Intermediate repairs on a 24 month cycle and 172,000 between Generals over a 48 month cycle. They were 'better' on these basic figures than almost any comparable type, though their duties were probably the least testing.

Concerning SIR JOHN... *British Railways Illustrated* **reader Alan Wild of Bournemouth comments on the following sequence of 30865 at Bournemouth.**

I have been unable to contact a friend who was a fireman at Bournemouth during the 1950s, and might have recognised some of the enginemen featured. However, Peter Smith, who was based at Branksome and thus was acquainted with some of the 'main line' men who worked to Bournemouth West, has looked at the prints. He pointed out that the fireman pulling coal forward on the tender is wearing a non-regulation flat cap; a hallmark of Nine Elms men in the pre-'knotted handkerchief' era.

The locomotive was shedded at Bournemouth through most, if not all, of the 1950s. With four beats-to-the-bar, SIR JOHN HAWKINS was regarded as the strongest member of the class. As the locomotive is clearly having a change of crew it must have come from Weymouth; the headcode will need to be changed before setting off for London. It cannot be a cross-country train as they always started from Bournemouth West and would not require to take water, or have coal pulled forward after only three miles! In any case inter-regional trains did not convey parcel vans.

In all probability the driver at the water column and his mate holding the 'bag' are Dorchester men. As indicated above, the relieving crew are most likely from Nine Elms although Bournemouth and Eastleigh men also swapped with Dorchester men on these turns. The position of the sun points to late morning. It was very unusual for van traffic to be conveyed on the fast trains, though almost every semi-fast had a Southern GUV behind the tender, as here. There was not normally a semi-fast from Weymouth to Waterloo at this time of day, so my guess is that the train is the 12.40pm express from Bournemouth (11.25am or thereabouts from Weymouth). A Bournemouth West portion would be attached to the rear while the locomotive was taking water. Peter Smith has a stock working book for the period which confirms that no van was scheduled to be conveyed on this train. Although most of the fast trains (which later became the two-hour services) were worked by Bulleid Pacifics during the mid-fifties, Lord Nelsons did appear regularly on one or two such diagrams.

A conceivable alternative is that the train is the summer Saturday 10.10am stopper from Weymouth to Waterloo, where the engine is not being changed at Bournemouth. This working only operated for a few years; it does not appear in the 1953 timetable and by 1959 it was 10.25 from Weymouth but only as far as Eastleigh. I can clearly recall a period when it did run to Waterloo, possibly 1955-57. That train usually comprised 4 or 5 coaches with vans at front and rear.

Detail on a Nelson; we don't know the exact date of these photographs of 30865 SIR JOHN HAWKINS but it would be in the first part of the 1950s, before March 1956, certainly, when it got 8 inch numbers – it has 10 inch in this sequence. The old sea dog is standing at Bournemouth Central and is more or less in final form, apart from some minor livery differences. I can state this with some confidence without being able to see the left-hand side, for this was the only Nelson that didn't get AWS or a speedometer. Photograph A.H. Lucas, The Transport Treasury.

Some fine lighting on SIR JOHN HAWKINS at Bournemouth. The old SR power classification, the 'A' was originally on the framing immediately behind the buffer beam but was repositioned early on in the BR regime below the cabside numerals, as here. Then the old LM-type system was adopted and the '7P' was duly applied above the numerals. It took a while for the redundant 'A' to disappear. Photograph A.H. Lucas, The Transport Treasury.

The tender lining in the BR livery cut across just below the point where the top of the tender side angled in, whereas in malachite it followed the tender outline – though some early dark green repaints actually maintained this. The somewhat ropy state of the tender sides is typical of the times; age, movement and corrosion began to show up the tender modification work of 1938-40. Photograph A.H. Lucas, The Transport Treasury.

Filling up SIR JOHN's tender and getting the coal forward for the job ahead. That tender certainly was 'a piece of work' as our American friends would put it; no wonder that, when the Schools 4-4-0s were found wanting in water capacity as the War went on, a number of Nine Elms Nelsons came to the rescue, including 865 itself. Photograph A.H. Lucas, The Transport Treasury.

That wonderful front end, showing to good effect the big chimney and the gap under the boiler at the front. The little hood alongside the front splasher (looking like a splasher itself) was actually a hinged cover to allow inspection and lubrication of the gear beneath, where pivot, radius rod and expansion link were joined. Photograph A.H. Lucas, The Transport Treasury.

No.850 LORD NELSON passing Birchington on Sea on the Thanet coast. There is no date but the 'No' has the 'dot' underneath which places it firmly in the 1930s; LORD NELSON got its modified cylinders in 1942, so it still has the 'piano' front.

Nine Elms, 21 May 1957. Notice that side wear has allowed the coupling rod to scrape the wheel boss. The only plate, naturally, not to have the additional LORD NELSON CLASS portion. Photograph J. Robertson, The Transport Treasury.

Typical train for a Nelson, a Salisbury 'stopper' at Vauxhall, 28 February 1959. 30850 now has the 'flat' front and the modified cylinders, which saw the steam pipes put out of sight behind the smoke deflectors. Photograph Frank Hornby.

The Eastleigh Nelson fleet provided a solid and reliable 'spine' for the services out of Waterloo to Southampton, Bournemouth and so on, the SR main lines being subject to seasonal peaks beyond that experienced elsewhere in Britain. On a hectic summer Saturday with everything going wrong, a big, solid powerful reliable steamer was the thing to have in a shedmaster's back pocket. There is no date or details for this photograph but it is Waterloo and the engine is in final condition about 1961 – note speedometer, second BR tender emblem, AWS battery box and the AWS conduit fixed to the left-hand running plate. Photograph Nigel Lester, The Transport Treasury.

LORD NELSON in its last full year, but still a stalwart of the 'Second Division' on the Southampton and Bournemouth lines, at Eastleigh shed on 15 August 1961. The engine was withdrawn in August the following year. LORD NELSON was preserved for the National Collection and spent a time based at Carnforth. It did some main line running, notably on the Cumbrian Mountain Express, putting up some lively performances and, it seems, transformed out of all recognition. While Prince Charles and Lady Diana Spencer were getting married in 1981 I was on the Settle & Carlisle behind 30850 in 'The Wedding Belle'. Currently undergoing overhaul at Eastleigh, it is hoped to be back on the main line in 2006. Photograph G.W. Morrison, The Transport Treasury.

E851 SIR FRANCIS DRAKE at Stewarts Lane (generally known as Battersea back then) in early condition, 18 April 1931. It has the smoke deflectors and the projecting lamp irons which, with the discs up, impaired forward visibility.

30851 SIR FRANCIS DRAKE at Eastleigh shed on 14 May 1949. The tender has the typical 'knocked about' look and SIR FRANCIS has the 'A' power classification but not yet the '7P'. It is wearing the post-war malachite green. Photograph J.H. Aston.

In BR green at where else but Eastleigh, 12 August 1955. SIR FRANCIS has the modified cylinders but these are the non-standard ones, fitted 'owing to a misunderstanding' – hence the continued presence of the old-style 'piano' at the front. Note how cylinder drain cock pipes clip into a fitting on the front steps. Eight inch numbers and shallow bogie frame. Photograph J. Robertson, The Transport Treasury.

SIR WALTER as E852 passing Vauxhall on 16 June 1931. Front lamp irons 'in-board' by now. The headcode indicates Waterloo to Southampton Terminus via Alton – and note the wonderful ancient LSWR stock. The photograph is a reminder that the Alton route was once an alternative line from Waterloo to Southampton with regular through services. Electrification to Alton put an end to this making it, from July 1937, a frontier with frequent electric trains from Waterloo and an infrequent steam service westwards provided by M7 tanks working push/pull. Photograph H.C. Casserley, courtesy R.M. Casserley.

30852 SIR WALTER RALEIGH on Eastleigh shed, 22 July 1958. Photograph B. Hilton, The Transport Treasury.

30853 SIR RICHARD GRENVILLE, cleaned and brewing up in determined style, in front of Eastleigh shed on 18 August 1950. This was the summer Saturday front line on the Southern and big reliable class 7 4-6-0s like the Nelsons would have been sorely missed had they gone early. SIR RICHARD GRENVILLE found itself one of only three (of those that got them) without the modified cylinders by the post-war period. It was in the end the last of that three to get them, in 1958. Photograph J.H. Aston.

Looking bonny in its dark BR garb, 30853 SIR RICHARD GRENVILLE (ten inch numbers) has a load well below its robust capabilities at Southampton Central, the 2.22pm stopping train for Bournemouth in May 1954. This Eastleigh duty involved the Nelson standing by at Southampton in the event of problems with the Pacific on the down Bournemouth Belle. Photograph S.C. Nash.

A shabby 30853 at Eastleigh shed in final form with AWS and associated holes in the lower left-hand cabside and speedometer, 29 September 1961. It has acquired that late addition, the removable panel on the cylinders. Photograph G.W. Morrison.

It's that spot again! See also Willie Hermiston's/John Robertson's efforts in *The Book of the Lord Nelson 4-6-0s* (page 34) for 30851 SIR FRANCIS DRAKE at this exact same spot, in very similar condition. 30853 SIR RICHARD GRENVILLE too, certainly provides an exceptional portrait at Eastleigh that day. In their later times a bolted/screwed patch appears on the Nelson cylinder casing. It obviously served some examination/access purpose and would appear to have become universal in the last year or two. Below, SIR RICHARD in altogether shabbier mode but, again, inevitably, at Eastleigh, 7 September 1961. Photographs W. Hermiston, The Transport Treasury and J.H. Aston.

No.854 HOWARD OF EFFINGHAM with 'a boat'; lamp irons 'in-board' by now. Photograph James Stevenson courtesy Hamish Stevenson.

A Nelson at its best. Malachite green and large chimney on 854 HOWARD OF EFFINGHAM; the year would almost certainly be 1939, when the chimney was fitted and the livery applied. Photograph W. Hermiston, The Transport Treasury.

Scintillating portrait of HOWARD OF EFFINGHAM alongside the great water tank at Eastleigh shed, looking super in the dark BR green, 25 July 1956. The engine was the one which had come off the line and fallen down the embankment in the Shawford accident of July 1952. Photograph The Transport Treasury.

30854 HOWARD OF EFFINGHAM at Eastleigh on 20 May 1957, fresh and shiny after a General completed only a week or so before. This would be the repair at which it got the second BR tender emblem. The plate has appeared on the cylinder casing. Photograph J. Robertson, The Transport Treasury.

Battered but unbowed, 30854 HOWARD OF EFFINGHAM stands at Eastleigh on 13 August 1961, weeks from withdrawal. The tender saw further service behind Schools 4-4-0 30921 SHREWSBURY. Photograph G.W. Morrison.

On 3 June 1952 30855 ROBERT BLAKE enters Basingstoke with an up local. It was a rapid fall from grace – as the 1930s came to an end the Nelsons were at something of a peak in their careers and there were credible instances of 100 mph exploits. Post-War it was very different. Photograph D.W. Winkworth.

30855 ROBERT BLAKE rolls into West Weybridge, 1 June 1953. Not long before this the curious Crewkerne near-disaster had taken place, leading to the withdrawal of the Merchant Navy Pacifics for axle investigations, then the checking of the light Pacifics. It was 7P V2s and Britannias that were drafted in rather than 'promoting' Nelsons and replacing them with Class 5s and there is nothing in the contemporary accounts of any particular 'starring role' for the Nelsons. Discs indicate Waterloo to Southampton Docks via East Putney. Photograph The Transport Treasury.

Two more of Jim Aston's 30855 ROBERT BLAKE in the down bay at Southampton Central, 6 June 1951 – see also *The Book of the Lord Nelson 4-6-0s*: 'I took it five times, it was such a sitting bird! A half-day cheap ticket Waterloo-Southampton was available that day on the 11.30 Waterloo. I didn't waste any time getting down on the track!' Ten inch numbers, which looked more appropriate for such a large loco than the later eight inch. Photographs J.H. Aston.

30855 ROBERT BLAKE in the unlikely surroundings of Basingstoke shed (an indication in itself of the 'Second Division' functions of the class, particularly by now) in September 1959. Winkworth sagely considers that, while all classes could only operate in their own times and circumstances and this influenced whether they were able to 'stand out' or not, relatively, the Nelsons were disproportionately affected by the times in which they found themselves. The years affording them the best opportunities were 1935-1939 with good track, improvements to the engines coming along and the best horsepower figures the class ever produced. Now what follows is only fancy (or 'a pointless comment' as Eric Youldon puts it, calling a spade a spade as usual) but if there had been fifty of them and the Merchant Navy Pacifics had never appeared, their 1950s work would have looked very different indeed. Photograph The Transport Treasury.

ROBERT BLAKE at Salisbury, October 1960; second BR tender emblem, AWS and speedometer. Photograph The Transport Treasury.

Looking doomed (as it indeed was) 30855 ROBERT BLAKE stands dumped at Eastleigh shed after withdrawal, 29 September 1961. Its right-hand handrail had certainly seen some last-minute excitement! That would be either 30854 HOWARD OF EFFINGHAM or 30858 LORD DUNCAN behind, also already withdrawn and waiting their own fate. Photograph G.W. Morrison.

856 LORD ST VINCENT at Stewarts Lane before the War; it was one of the four turned out with stovepipe chimneys for exhaust experiments together with this olive (or 'Dover') green livery. Nos.855 and 861 had modified tenders with the high sides and had the SOUTHERN in line with the cab numbers. In the case of 856 and 863, however, they still had their straight sided tenders at the time and the SOUTHERN was placed lower down than the cab number, as here. Note Flaman speed recorder, piano front, old pattern cylinders and power classification 'A' on running frame behind buffer beam. Photograph The Transport Treasury.

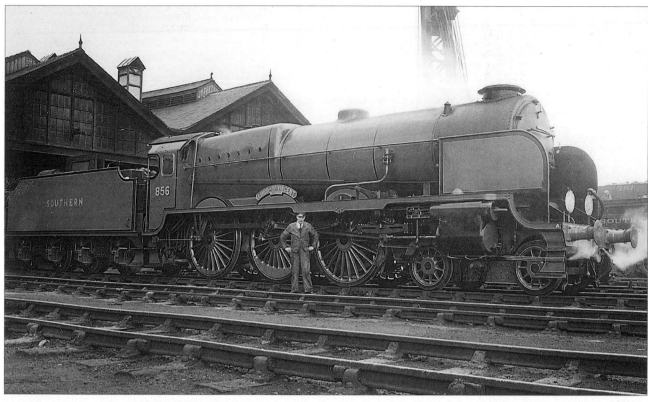

Less than a year later LORD ST VINCENT now has the standard Lemaître chimney and the malachite green (smoke deflector panel prominent). The location looks like the big engine shed at Salisbury. Photograph collection Hamish Stevenson.

LORD ST VINCENT with a train at Southampton, May 1958, in very different condition. 'Seldom did any' of the work performed by the Nelsons post-war 'give the opportunity for performance heroics' is how Winkworth characterises the work of the class in BR days, with admirable economy. Photograph Jack A.C. Kirke.

Two Nelsons at Eastleigh on 2 May 1962, 30856 LORD ST VINCENT (top) and 30857 LORD HOWE, AWS battery box and speedometer prominent in both cases. But look again – there are always more details that come to light. The AWS battery boxes, it turns out, had two different positions on the left-hand running plate. Until about August 1960 the box, when fitted, sat between the middle and rear splasher (see LORD HOWE below). After that, when boxes were fitted they were positioned alongside the rear splasher, as in LORD ST VINCENT's case. We think of the heyday of the Nelsons ending at the start of World War Two and so it did in the sense that it was possible to *observe* the said heyday. Much of railway operation disappeared from the photographic record from 1939 till film was generally available some time after war's end. More likely it was 1949 that saw the final termination of the Nelsons as a frontline force. The drift to Eastleigh commenced and from there their work, it could be said, was comprised of four distinct types. These were boat trains ('the boats'), a handful (four actually) of regular top link rosters and what might be termed 'others'; that is, excursions, specials and freights such as fitted banana specials from the Docks. The fourth category was the summer Saturday extra when they were certainly out in force, but these amounted to only a dozen or so days out of 365. There was thus, undeniably, a deal of slack in the class at Eastleigh and on a winter Saturday almost half would be idle. The small stud at Bournemouth until 1959 (30860, 30864 and 30865) could be found regularly on the Oxfords. Photographs John Scrace.

857 LORD HOWE at Salisbury shed with the taper boiler, probably in 1937; it first bore the boiler from January that year through to 1941 and again from January 1943 to February 1945. Note the odd deflectors. Photograph The Transport Treasury.

LORD HOWE at Bromley, 30 March 1938. The boiler was said to be a precursor for a Maunsell Pacific or goods 4-8-0, though 'at the time', Winkworth notes, 'some play was made of it being an improvement to the Lord Nelson class'. It was said to steam more freely than the conventional Nelsons, except when driven hard. Townroe concluded that the draughting was wrong and that 'further experiments were needed with the blastpipe and chimney' but these never materialised. Maunsell retired the following year and Bulleid apparently had no interest in LORD HOWE's strange boiler. Single snifting valve behind chimney. Photograph H.C. Casserley, courtesy R.M. Casserley.

LORD HOWE in close-up, at Basingstoke about 1948, carrying a normal Lord Nelson boiler. Photograph Brian H. Fletcher, The Transport Treasury.

LORD HOWE in malachite at Nine Elms, 15 June 1946. Photograph H.C. Casserley, courtesy R.M. Casserley.

Headboard experiments at Eastleigh in the 1950s. This was the only Nelson to get the first emblem in its small version as here – applied 7/52 and removed 2/55.

Bournemouth, 19 July 1951; BR green and with the 'A' classification under the number. The '7P' has yet to appear. As this was an early dark green Nelson, the tender lining is taken to top of the curved section and the valance lining follows true contour. Emblem is in high position. Photograph The Transport Treasury.

E858 LORD DUNCAN near Petts Wood, 28 March 1929 – Urie tender with auxiliary vacuum reservoirs. Photograph H.C. Casserley, courtesy R.M. Casserley.

LORD DUNCAN at Eastleigh, newly garbed in BR green, 2 June 1951. It carries a Nine Elms 70A plate and had been there since before the War; it did not gravitate to Eastleigh where the class was latterly concentrated until 1958. Emblem is high although lining is low. Photograph F.A. Wycherley.

With the tender starting to acquire the familiar wonkiness, LORD DUNCAN stands at Nine Elms on 17 August 1956. Photograph W. Hermiston, The Transport Treasury.

An up Bournemouth express behind 30859 LORD HOOD at Malden, 11.45am on 4 December 1955. LORD HOOD was the Nelson with the smaller driving wheels though it is very difficult to tell – impossible in a view like this. Photograph Alan Lathey, The Transport Treasury.

Woebegone at Eastleigh, 15 August 1961, though it was not withdrawn until the end of the year. Muliple jet blast pipe removed and deposited on front platform. The remarkable thing is that the Nelsons lasted as long as they did, only a year or so short of the first withdrawals of East and West Coast Pacifics and various others that performed far grander work throughout the 1950s. It's especially impressive as there never was a general reboilering. Townroe considered them obsolescent even in 1948 'and quite obsolescent alongside the excellent BR Class 5s, easily serviced and maintained'. Photograph G.W. Morrison.

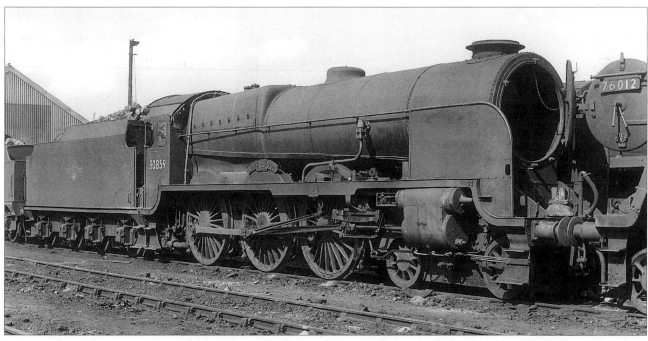

30859 LORD HOOD at Southampton Docks on 26 June 1957. This was a typical working for a Nelson, an Ocean Liner Express – in this case for the Greek Line ship 'Neptune'. Photograph R.C. Riley, The Transport Treasury.

LORD HAWKE with an E prefix on the tender, in original livery and with Urie pattern tender, at Clapham Junction. The latter was replaced in May 1931. It was the last of the main batch of ten and as such the last to be built without deflectors. The last five which came after, 861-865, had the deflectors from new. Photograph The Transport Treasury.

E860 LORD HAWKE at Waterloo after about the middle of 1932. LORD HAWKE was the one with the longer boiler, so there is no 'piano' front. Photograph The Transport Treasury.

Now in malachite green, at Bournemouth shed. The date is not known but 860 went into malachite 12/39 and the Q 0-6-0 537 lost its Maunsell livery (shown here) 12/42 so the picture was taken between those dates, probably in early 1940. Photograph The Transport Treasury.

Not too long afterwards, 30860 LORD HAWKE in its new guise, again at Bournemouth shed, with BR numbers and letters though still in malachite. In the shed yard another Nelson, similarly brilliantly shined, lurks. The period from the end of the war to 1949 certainly saw a profound change in the circumstances of the class. In 1939 the Nelsons had been to the fore, increasingly so, but once Pacifics were available in quantities their sphere of operations shrank markedly. Photograph courtesy Hamish Stevenson.

LORD HAWKE on The Cunarder, a favourite and mainly Pullman boat train for the class, at Clapham Junction with the up train on 25 July 1956. The concentration of Nelsons at Eastleigh provided a pool of suitable engines for all these varied boat workings. They might be obsolescent, as Townroe pointed out, but they could poodle about in the week and rise to the boat train occasion as necessary. Photograph Brian Morrison.

Approaching Vauxhall on 19 May 1956 30860 LORD HAWKE has (photographer Peter Groom was convinced) the 10.30am Waterloo-Bournemouth. The headcode is correct for this, but it has been pointed out that it is a 'SPL' – Special. The picture was once used on the cover of an Ian Allan 'ABC'. Photograph Peter Groom.

At Nine Elms, in the old bomb-ruined part of the shed, on 5 May 1956, among much later Western Section stars, decades later than LORD HAWKE, the mighty victor of Quiberon Bay. It was the Southern summer peak that ensured the Nelsons' survival, allied to the sometimes unpredictable availability (or at least the perception thereof) of the Pacifics. 30860 has a standard boiler by this time. Photograph A.R. Carpenter, The Transport Treasury.

In unnatural company. LORD HAWKE at Waterloo in August 1961. It was withdrawn exactly a year later. Photograph Brian H. Fletcher, The Transport Treasury.

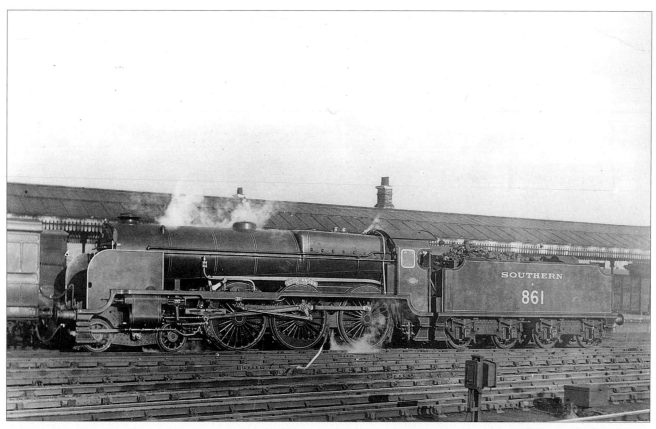

E861 LORD ANSON making up a job with empty stock at Clapham Junction, 23 November 1930, in the lovely original livery that included lining to the cylinders, steps and even the 'splasher' (it can *just* be made out) over the trailing pair of wheels on the bogie. Photograph H.C. Casserley, courtesy R.M. Casserley.

Down Bournemouth train at Vauxhall, 2.45pm on 16 July 1955. If Townroe is interpreted literally (though one wouldn't want to sound biblical about this) the Nelsons were in effect a reserve pool, for on any particular day the number of Pacifics available for service might fluctuate widely. 'On paper' he writes, there was 'little justification for keeping so many Arthurs and Nelsons' Photograph Alan Lathey, The Transport Treasury.

Above. Gavin Morrison managed to catch most of the Nelsons at Eastleigh, on family visits during this period. Still a highly impressive machine, 30861 LORD ANSON with patched-up smoke deflector makes a very fine figure at Eastleigh shed on 17 August 1961, its last full working year. LORD ANSON was party to coal consumption trials under Bulleid in 1946, along with 21C14 NEDERLAND LINE and 789 SIR GUY. The Nelson returned a little under 45lbs per mile, more or less what was expected of a Nelson at the time but Bradley makes the fascinating historical point, given the associations of the Lord Nelson design with that of the Royal Scots, that LORD ANSON's figures were almost exactly comparable to the LM's 46154 THE HUSSAR in the BR locomotive exchanges eighteen months or so later. Photograph G.W. Morrison. *Inset*. Eastleigh, 20 May 1957. It doesn't do to look at paintwork too closely! Photograph J. Robertson, The Transport Treasury.

30862 LORD COLLINGWOOD on 7 August 1948 immediately ex-works at Eastleigh (there is a Schools to the right and fellow Nelson 30865 behind) shiny and sleek in new malachite green with the intermediate BRITISH RAILWAYS on the tender – painted over without smoothing out the dints and warps. This was the last Nelson to go green from black post-war. Photograph J.H. Aston.

Travel-stained 30862 LORD COLLINGWOOD departs Bournemouth Central for Waterloo about 1956-57. Photograph T.R. Smith, The Transport Treasury.

30862 LORD COLLINGWOOD on the 3.20pm Waterloo-Bournemouth train at Brockenhurst, 26 June 1954. Photograph R.C. Riley, The Transport Treasury.

30862 LORD COLLINGWOOD at Nine Elms, 21 May 1957. It shows well the curved cover over the pivot/ expansion link which was open at one end (the forward end) and hinged at the other for easy access. The opening was simply the handhold. More elusive features include the sand pipe (only the front drivers had sanding) running down and the almost never seen filler cap above; also the 'splasher' over the rear bogie wheel. Noting its thick coat of grease it is hard to imagine that it was once painted *and* lined! The view emphasises the extra long piston rod, and slidebar pattern adopted by Bulleid for his Pacifics. Linkage for the drain cocks can be traced. Photograph J. Robertson, The Transport Treasury.

Nine Elms, 21 May 1957. Photograph J. Robertson, The Transport Treasury.

A proud old Driver on 30863 LORD RODNEY at Oxford, 21 April 1956. It has just arrived and will shortly move forward to the shed for turning. This was a Saturday, if not quite a summer one, and while the Nelsons might be trundling around in the week, it was certainly the summer Saturdays which saw them come into their own. Bradley makes the surprising claim that 'it was not uncommon' to observe all sixteen of them at work on such days, ranging from Waterloo-Bournemouth expresses to trains such as this, bound for other BR Regions. A Nelson was 'automatically substituted' if the Merchant Navy on the 'Belle' happened to fail. The vertical 'tube' on the tender side is interesting. A tap inside the tender could be turned on and water rose up the external tube which had a series of holes in it. The highest 'leak' showed roughly how full the tender was. Crude, but effective! Photograph R.C. Riley, The Transport Treasury.

30863 LORD RODNEY at Eastleigh shed on 8 May 1960. This was the one that kept its Maunsell cylinders, hence the survival of the 'piano' front and the steam pipes projecting through the smoke deflectors. AWS cabside holes clearly shown; second BR tender emblem. Photograph Peter Groom.

Gavin Morrison and, once again, a Nelson in its dotage, 17 August 1961. Its end came in February the following year, hitched up to an engineer's train from Hither Green to Tonbridge, cruelly making LORD RODNEY work to its final resting place, Ashford works. LORD RODNEY might look tired but you can still see it taking over from a Merchant Navy for the run up to London if needed, and maybe even keeping time! AWS but no speedometer (it never got one). Photograph G.W. Morrison.

One of the few examples I could find of a Nelson in black – though you'd hardly know from the wartime grime on 864 SIR MARTIN FROBISHER, at Nine Elms on 15 June 1946. It was later one of the Nelsons to get the short-lived apple green. Photograph H.C. Casserley, courtesy R.M. Casserley.

30864 SIR MARTIN FROBISHER at Brockenhurst on 11 September 1953; it was one of two Nelsons (the other was 30865) that worked from Dorchester shed for a few months in 1954. The grandest engines on the complement, they were kept clean and respectable and for the summer of that year were rostered to two morning Weymouth-Waterloo trains and their afternoon returns to Bournemouth West. Photograph R.C. Riley, The Transport Treasury.

Clapham Cutting, and 30864 SIR MARTIN FROBISHER hurries through on 24 May 1958. Photograph The Transport Treasury.

Running through Basingstoke, 1 August 1953. The Engine Records only imperfectly record many modifications and often do not record them at all. Reflecting their value to the Running Department, perhaps, a number of Nelsons got manganese axlebox liners, water treatment and regulator/injector modifications. The last five, 30861-30865, even got drop grates, though I'm unaware of any external indications of these features. Photograph The Transport Treasury.

30864 SIR MARTIN FROBISHER at Nine Elms in September 1960. Photograph D.H. Beecroft, The Transport Treasury.

E865 SIR JOHN HAWKINS filling-in on empty stock at Clapham Junction, 25 January 1931. Photograph H.C. Casserley, courtesy R.M. Casserley.

With the 'E' gone, SIR JOHN at Waterloo has the 'No.' on the buffer beam, with the 'dot' under the line which, despite modern technology, seems impossible to reproduce.

Malachite green the first time, within days of its application, on 865 SIR JOHN HAWKINS at Waterloo in June 1939. The 'water level tube' is conspicuous on the tender side and the rear tender detail is useful. Compare with the old sea dog at Nine Elms in the first malachite (*The Book of the Lord Nelson 4-6-0s*, p24); the main difference is that here the tender is as yet not modified by extension to the sides. Early Bulleid number and ledgend. Photograph K. Pullen, The Transport Treasury.

SIR JOHN amid the remains of the coal stage at Nine Elms, in BR green, 17 August 1956. A cousin to Francis Drake, 'Jack' Hawkins possibly played an even more important role in saving England from the Spanish, though he is always associated with the slave trade. He furnished the Navy with fighting machines 'technologically superior' to those of the Spanish. The Nelsons might not have been 'technologically superior' to the engines around them and the engines that came after but they certainly played their part in the fleet. Photograph J. Robertson, The Transport Treasury.

The following table is made up from a more comprehensive one first set out by D.W. Winkworth in *Maunsell's Nelsons* and subsequently amended in the light of later discoveries (personally communicated by Mr D.W. Winkworth and Mr E.S. Youldon, for which many thanks).

No.	850	851	852	853	854	855	856	857	858	859	860	861	862	863	864	865
Built	8/26	6/28	7/28c	9/28D	10/28	11/28	12/28	12/28R	2/29E	3/29E	4/29F	9/29	10/29K	10/29	11/29	11/29K
Tender modified	6/39	6/39	11/37	10/40	2/39	8/38	7/40	10/39	5/40	1/40	12/39	11/38	4/40	12/40	11/38	9/40
Flaman recorder	9/38	6/39	4/39	4/39	2/39	8/38	11/38	10/38	5/39	11/38	12/39	11/38	10/38	11/38	11/38H	6/39
Olive Green	-	-	4/39	-	2/39	11/38H	11/38H	-	5/39	5/39	-	11/38H	-	11/38	-	-
Lemaître exhaust	6/39	6/39	4/39	4/39	6/39	9/39L	8/39L	10/39	5/39	5/39	12/39	10/39L	5/39	6/39M	6/39L	6/39
Malachite Green	6/39	6/39	-	4/39	6/39	9/39	8/39	10/39	5/40	1/40	12/39	10/39	5/39	6/39	6/39	6/39
Modified cyl.	3/42	6/39N	3/40	2/58	11/46	12/40	7/40	10/39	1/51	12/46	12/39	8/43	4/40	-	5/48	9/40
Black livery	4/44	1/44	6/42	2/43	12/43	4/43	9/42	1/43	9/42	5/42	10/42	8/43	7/43	11/42	6/43	5/43
Malachite Green	11/46	11/46	3/47	6/47	11/46	5/47	6/46A	6/46	3/46	12/46	1/47	11/47A	8/48	9/46	2/47A	6/46
S. V. removed	11/48	1/49	3/49	11/48	6/49	2/49	4/48	12/49	1/48	1/48	11/48	11/47	8/48	11/47	5/48	8/48
BR renumbering	11/48	1/49	3/49	11/48	6/49B	2/49	4/48	12/49	6/48	2/49	11/48	5/48	8/48	8/49	5/48	8/48
BR Green	1/51	10/50	12/51	7/50	10/51	9/50	4/50	12/49	1/51	3/51	10/50	3/50	2/51	8/49	4/51	11/49
AWS gear	12/60	9/60	8/60	4/60	10/59	6/60	9/60	7/60	10/59	9/59	12/60	12/59	5/61	10/59	10/59	-
Speedometer	12/60	9/60	8/60	4/60	-	6/60	9/60	7/60	-	-	12/60	12/59	5/61	-	-	-
Withdrawn	8/62	12/61	2/62	3/62	9/61T	9/61	9/62	9/62	8/61	12/61	8/62	10/62	10/62	2/62	1/62	5/61T
Cut up	P	5/62	2/62	4/62	9/61	2/62	11/62	10/62	11/61	12/61	8/62	11/62	10/62	2/62	3/62	8/61

A – Apple-green livery acquired 30856 in 6/48, 30861/4 in 5/48
B – 'S' prefix 3/48
C – Six-wheel tender until 11/29 and Urie-type tender until 6/32
D – Six-wheel tender until 1/30 and Urie-type tender until 2/32
E – Urie-type tender until 6/32
F – Urie-type tender until 5/31 and fitted with longer boiler (no 860)
H – Fitted with large-diameter chimney and involved in exhaust experiments
K – Kylchap-type exhaust and double chimney fitted (no 862 in 8/34 and no 865 in 3/38)
L – Fitted with standard Lemaître exhaust and large-diameter chimney
M – Fitted with large-diameter chimney and involved in exhaust experiments 6/38
N – Non-standard modified cylinders
P – Preserved
R – Non-Belpaire boiler (no 1063) fitted from 1/37 to 9/41 and from 1/43 to 2/45
T – Tender 1007 from no 30854 transferred to no 30921 and tender 1012 from no 30865 to no 30912
S.V.- Snifting Valves